J 793.7 35
T36   77-131

Thaler, Mike
Soup with Crackers

Chanute Public Library
Chanute, Kansas 66720

SOUP WITH QUACKERS!

SOUP WITH QUACKERS

FUNNY CARTOON RIDDLES

by Mike Thaler, the creator of Letterman

FRANKLIN WATTS | NEW YORK | LONDON | 1976

Copyright © 1976 by Michael C. Thaler
All rights reserved
Printed in the United States of America

6 5 4 3 2 1

Library of Congress Cataloging in Publication Data

Thaler, Mike, 1936–
   Soup with quackers!

   SUMMARY: Collection of riddles illustrated with cartoon drawings.
   1. Riddles—Juvenile literature. [1. Riddles] I. Title.
PN6371.T5   398.6   76–10308
ISBN 0-531-00344-2

For Mr. P., who hates riddles

What's the noisiest way to eat soup?

With quackers!

What kind of train sneezes the most?

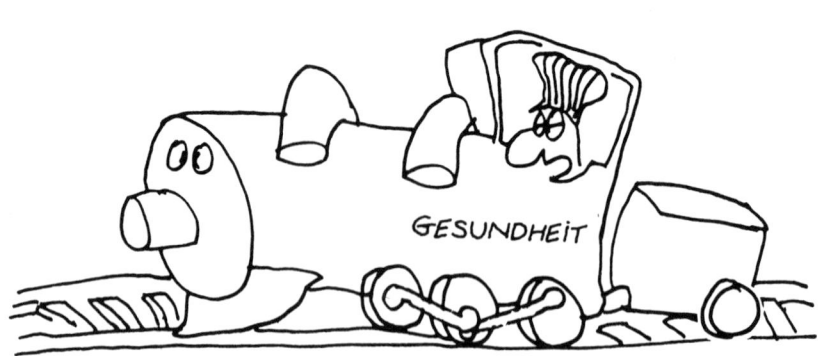

Ah choo choo train.

When do astronauts eat?

At launch time.

When does a car look like a frog?

When it's being toad.

What Russian city has the most mice?

Mouscow.

With what big cat should you never play cards?

A cheetah.

What Chinese leader can lick the most stamps?

Mao Tse-tongue.

What has eight legs, lives at the bottom of the ocean, and says "Meow"?

An octapussy.

What has long hair, wears beads, and weighs 2,000 pounds?

A hippie-potamus.

What do you call a baby sheep who swallows a light bulb?

A lamp.

What was a favorite sport during the Middle Ages?

Serfing.

What player on a baseball team can hold the most milk?

The pitcher.

What state has the most cows?

What do Hungarians wear when it rains?

Goulashes.

What mouse was the Emperor of Rome?

Julius Cheeser.

What do you call a flea who lives on a French poodle?

A Paris-ite.

What kind of car does a rich cat drive?

A Cat-illac.

What kind of car does a rich baker drive?

An Onion Rolls.

What do you call the king of
Russian sardines?

The Czardine.

What always sleeps through dinner?

The napkins.

Where's the last place Indians get dessert?

What is it called when an automobile writes a book about itself?

An autobiography.

How do you make an engine obey?

Train it.

What kind of table can you swim in?

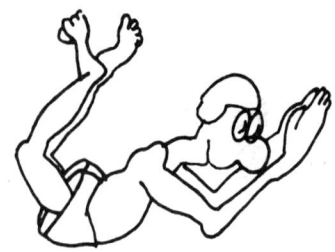

A pool table.

Why did the otter cross the road?

To get to the otter side.

What famous chicken crossed the Alps?

Hennibal.

What's the fastest coffee in the world?

Expresso.

What color do people turn when they are left on desert islands?

Maroon.

What animals do bald men like best?

Hares.

Who's the toughest can in the world?

Genghis Can.

What do you call pigs who write letters to each other?

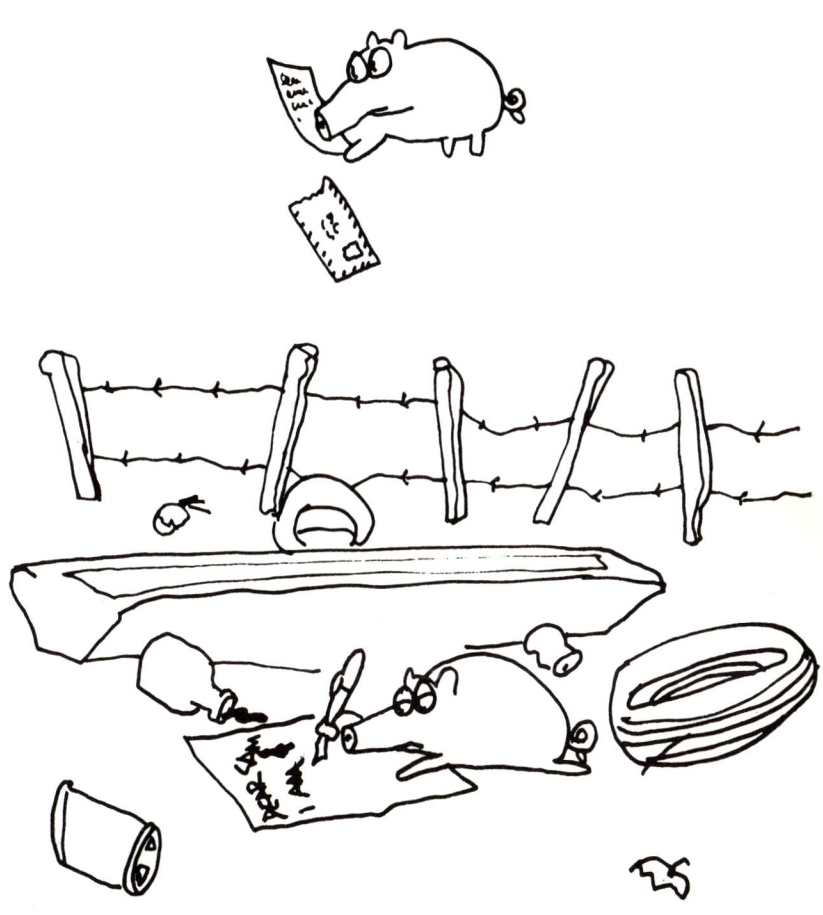

Pen pals.

What is it called when a king climbs a mountain?

Hiking.

How do you cross a moat?

In a moater boat.

How many ants can fit in a boardinghouse?

Tenants.

Where do cows go on dates?

Moooovies.

What President did the most laundry?

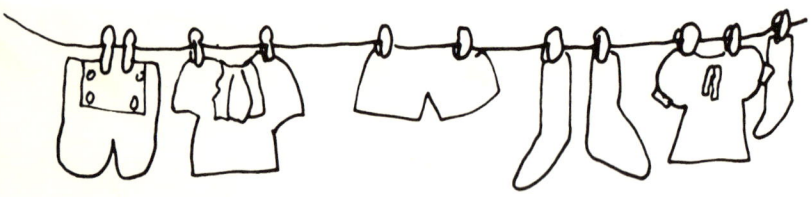

Washington.

What cat was the most famous artist in the twentieth century?

Picatso.

What kind of camel makes the most noise?

A drumedary.

What do you call a clean gangster?

A mopster.

What's the heaviest soup in the world?

Won ton.

What's the cheapest way to buy holes?

Hole sale.

What's it called when three pears march down the street?

A pearade.

What does a deaf fish need?

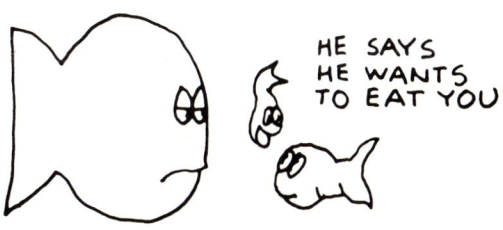

A herring aid.

What tribe of Indians are the best lawyers?

The Sue.

What do you call an elephant
that goes up and down?

An elephator.

What's the most difficult stool to sit on?

A toadstool.

What do you get when you cross
a crocodile and an abalone?

A crock-a-baloney.

What kind of melon can't run away and get married?

A cantaloupe.

What's the smartest kind of bean?

A human bean.

What's it like to live in a house with nine bears?

What's it called when a lot of stamps run out of the post office?

A stampede.

What's the biggest potato in the world?

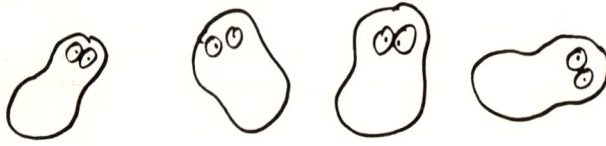

A hip-potato-mus.

What big cat helps people when they do their laundry?

A clothes lion.

What do ghosts wear on their feet?

Boooooots.

How did Edison feel when he invented the electric bulb?

Delighted.

What kind of bows can't be put in your hair?

Oboes, elbows, hobos, gazebos, and rainbows.

What kind of nuts sneeze the most?

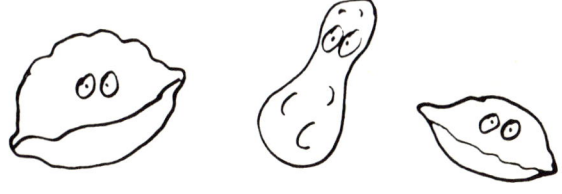

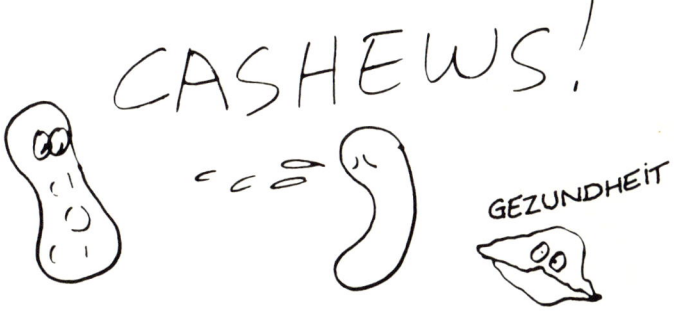

What game do crows like best?

Croquet.

What are the hardest things to walk in?

Slippers.

Who was the greatest Indian card player?

Poker-hontas.

What color is a happy cat?

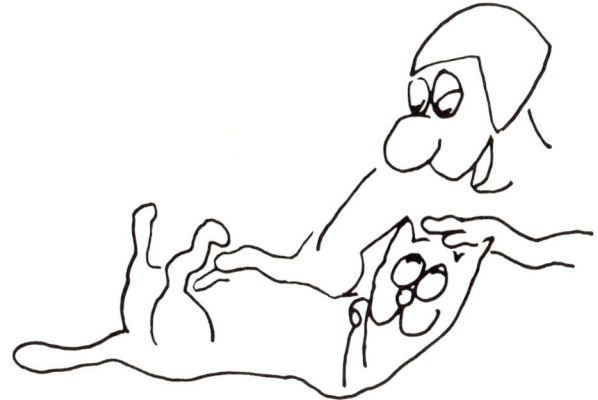

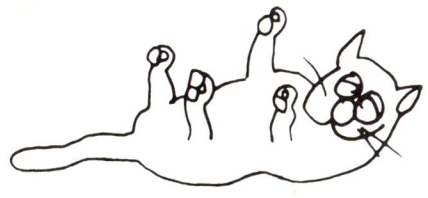

Purrrrrrple.

What is it called when an animal with a long neck writes on a wall?

Giraffiti.

Who was the meanest goat in the West?

Billy the Kid.

Who is the leader of the Chinese cats?

Meow Tse-tung.

What instrument makes the most sour notes?

A pickle-o.

What do you call three trees playing music?

A trio.

What is it called when a sheepdog has a lot of wives?

A hair-em.

What storybook kingdom had the most camels?

Camelot.

What tower in France is hard to look at all at once?

The Eyeful Tower.

What is a lamb chop called if you use it to row through space?

A meaty oar.

What celestial body has the most cows?

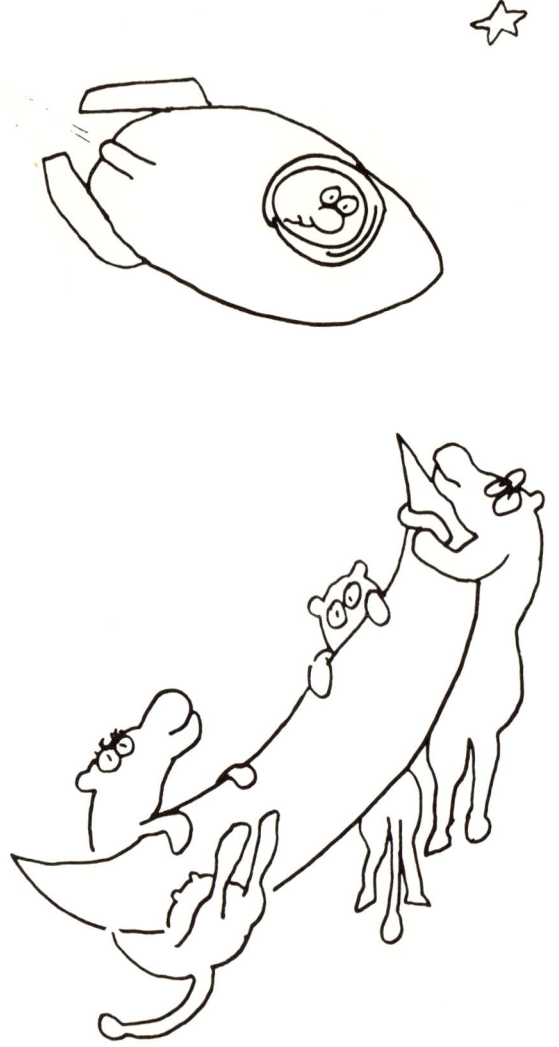

The mooooon.

What do you call it when a walrus eats 1,000 clams?

A clamity!

What is the most unusual vegetable?

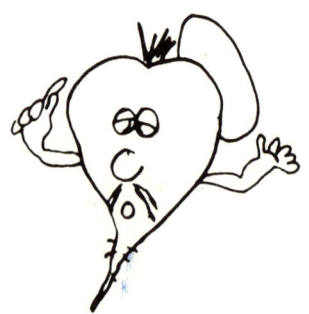

A beetnik.

What's the toughest vegetable in the world?

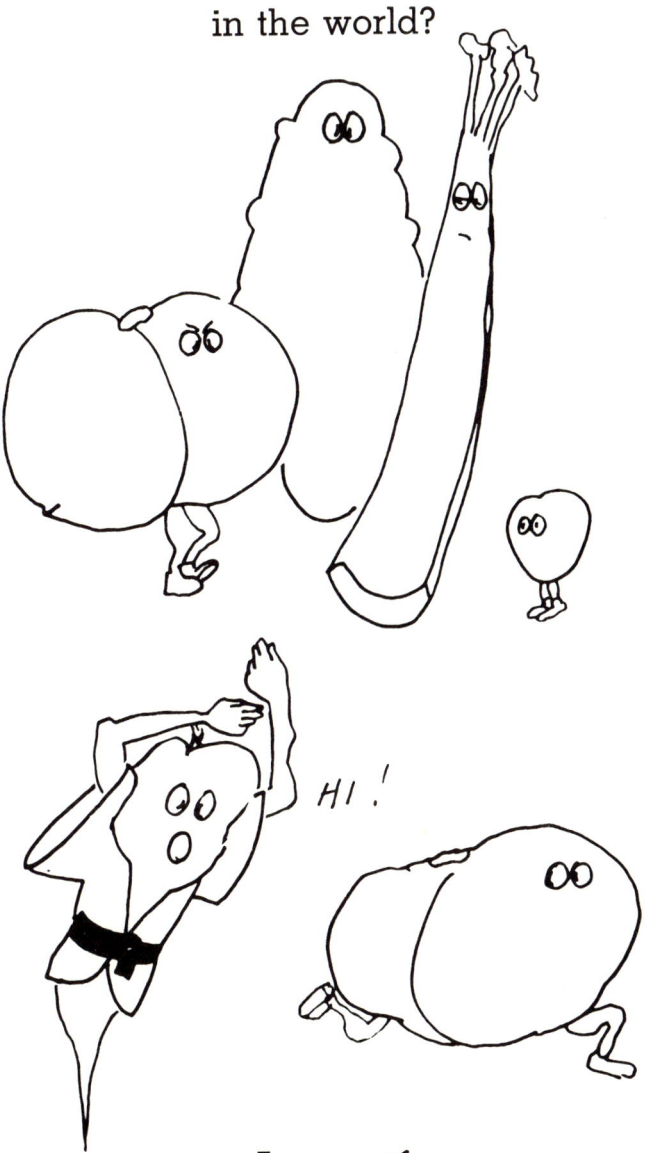

A carroté.

How do you get a shellfish upstairs?

Oyster up.

What do you call Italian noblemen who fight over money?

Charge accounts.

What pear was a famous playwright?

William Shakespear.

Why can't kings sit in chairs?

Because they always get a throne.

What is it called when chickens dance outside the third base line?

What state has the most pigs?

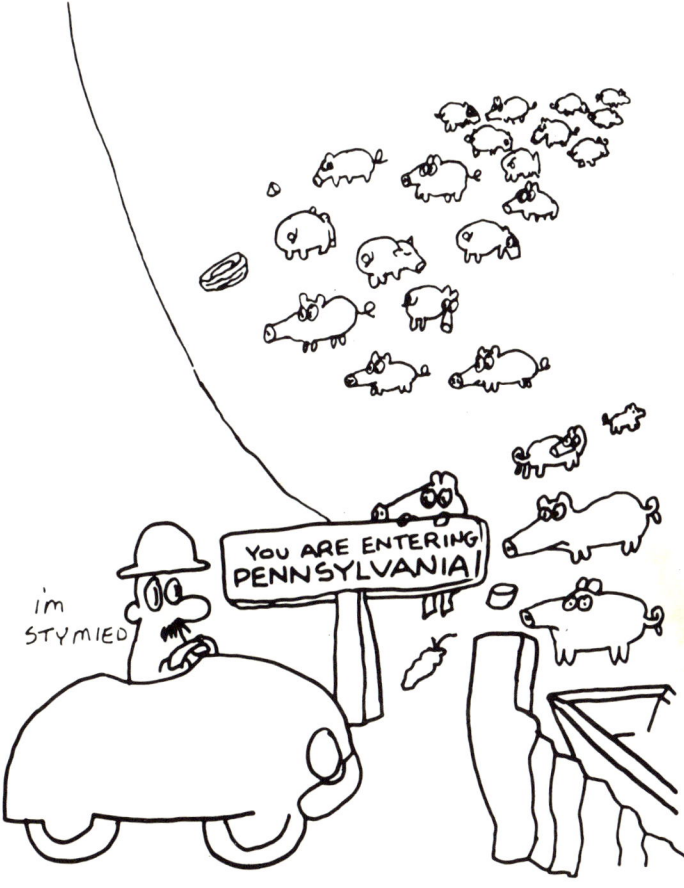

What kind of cracker should never be put into soup?

A firecracker.

What's it like living under a carpet?

It's very rugged.

What fruit do gorillas sleep on at camp?

Apricots.

What fish can fix a piano?

A tuna.

What kind of cycle is very hard to ride?

A popsicle.

In what country can you never win?

Thailand.

Where does a shrimp borrow money?

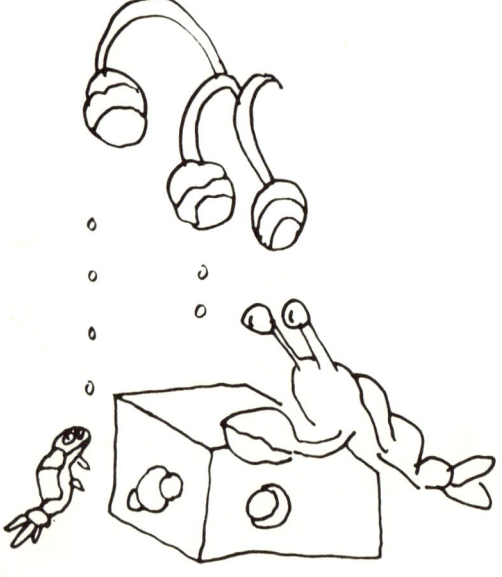

A prawn shop.

What car makes the line down a road disappear?

A-racer.

ABOUT THE AUTHOR

Mike Thaler rarely goes anywhere without his notebook and pencil to jot down the wild assortment of riddles that continually pop into his head and that have made him a favorite with children. Among his many other talents, Mr. Thaler is a cartoonist, teacher, sculptor, and songwriter. He is also the creator of Letterman, the popular cartoon character seen on The Electric Company.